The Ten Dad Commandments

Fatherhood Through the Lens of Hip-Hop

Esteban A. Serrano

MP MAHAL PUBLISHING

Mahal Publishing

PODCAST°

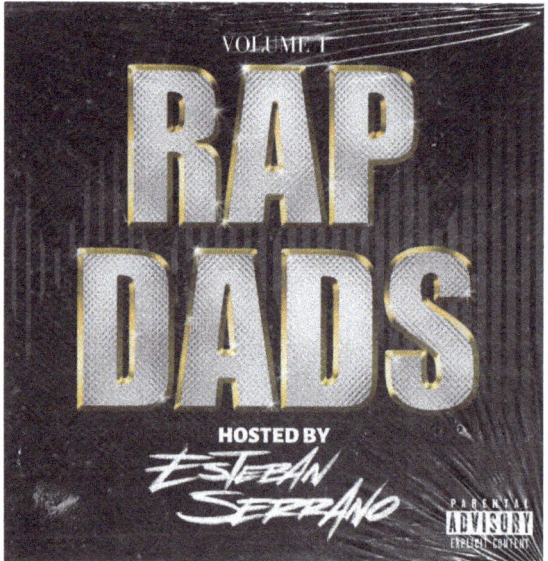

VOLUME 1

RAP DADS

HOSTED BY
ESTEBAN SERRANO

PARENTAL
ADVISORY
EXPLICIT CONTENT

STREAMING ON ALL PLATFORMS

NOW

THE RAP DADS PLATFORM IS A PLACE WHERE THE HIP-HOP COMMUNITY CAN BAND TOGETHER AND LEARN/TEACH EACH OTHER ABOUT THE MOST IMPORTANT ROLE WE WILL PLAY IN OUR LIVES, FATHERHOOD.

Contents

ABOUT THE AUTHOR   1

DEDICATION   4

FORWARD   6

MESSAGE TO NEW FATHERS   9

MESSAGE TO STEP-FATHERS   11

THE INTRO   13

1. KNOW YOUR ROLE (WHAT IS A FATHER?)   16

2. WATCH THE COMPANY YOU KEEP   27

3. PROTECT   33

4. ACTION! GET INVOLVED   48

5. LOVE, EMPATHY & COMPASSION   57

6. LEAD BY EXAMPLE   72

7. DISCIPLINE   79

8. BE HUMAN   86

9. KEEP AN OPEN MIND   91

10. HAVE FAITH   97

ABOUT THE AUTHOR

What Up RAP DADS! My name is Esteban Serrano. I'm a West Philadelphia born and raised husband and father of three sons.

Professionally I'm a TV/Film producer and director. For more than nineteen years of my career I've worked in music television for networks like MTV, BET & FUSE. Throughout my career my favorite conversations with artists and celebrities have been about fatherhood. It's been an exciting and challenging subject to tackle. But one thing I've noticed is the enthusiasm artists have about the role of being a father.

My fatherhood journey began when I was twenty two years old and I fell in love with my best friend and now wife who had a one year old son. This thrusted me into the role of a "step-father." Two years later we had another son and three years after that the trilogy was complete!

My unique experiences in fatherhood make it easy for me to speak to the many different circumstances that come with the responsibility.

I also love to draw and learn from my own upbringing. I was blessed to be raised by a RAP DAD. He loved Hip-Hop and he loved me. When I was really young, my mom and dad were not together. I was able to experience what it's like being a young kid who didn't always have access to his father. I also got to experience what lengths my dad would go through to make sure I was taken care of and that I knew how much he loved me.

Eventually, when I was nine years old, my mother and father got married. I then got to experience having my dad live with me full time. So much of my own childhood helps to shape how I parent. This is also why the first question on my RAP DADS podcast is usually about the relationship my guest had with their own father. It truly helps to inform a lot about their style whether they realize it or not.

Believe it or not, your fatherhood journey didn't start when you became a father yourself but it started with your own relationship with your father. Good or Bad it is your first point of reference.

Nowadays (at the time of writing this book) my sons are nineteen, sixteen & thirteen years old. My oldest is in college at Drexel University on a scholarship. My middle son, my clone, is a rock star and a skateboarder. My youngest son, my best work, is going to be an amazing television producer one day, like his dad, he just doesn't know it yet. But most importantly they are amazing, thoughtful, caring, positive, confident young men. At the end of the day I can sit back and say I contributed some dope people to this world. Ain't that the goal!?!?

DEDICATION

This book is dedicated to my village. To the many men who helped mold me into a man. My uncles, both biological and play. My big cousins Gene & Eric. My OGs Sway Calloway, Eric Clark, Sekou, Gio, Stang and Sean Williams. To my imaginary mentors like Rev Run, Dr. Heathclif Huxtable, Uncle Phil, Roc and them. To my Dads Got Kicks Podcast homies and Swagger Dad.

Above all it's dedicated to my hero, my dad Steve Serrano. Throughout this book you will read about the many lessons he taught me by example. My dad was the only present father in my neighborhood so I got to see first hand how important that position is in a kid's life.

I also want to dedicate this book to my sons; Josyah, Esteban & Mikael. Thank you for choosing me to be your dad and knowing that I would step up and give you my best. You guys have taught me so much about myself it's unbelievable. You are the reason I'm writing this book. One, I want to make sure I embody these commandments. And two, I also want to leave you with a wealth of knowledge to learn from when you become fathers!

Last but not least I want to thank my Rapper dad mentors out there. This book is a play on a track by the Notorious B.I.G. On one of his very first tracks, Juicy, he made it very clear how proud he was to be a father. Before he even started rapping he let you know he was just trying to make some money to feed his daughter. So shout out to the amazing RAP DADS out there making it fly to take care of your kids.

FORWARD

IF YOU'RE READING THIS, IT'S <u>NOT</u> TOO LATE

Dear Reader,

As a father, one of the most important roles we play in life is guiding and shaping the next generation. It is a role that comes with great responsibility, but also great reward. In "The Ten Dad Commandments," you will find a roadmap for navigating the complexities of fatherhood and becoming the best father you can be.

This book offers practical advice and wisdom on how to lead with love and integrity, how to instill values in your children, and how to be present and engaged in their lives. It is a must-read for any father looking to not only fulfill his duties as a parent, but also to enrich and enhance the lives of his children.

I was inspired to write this book after the countless conversations I had with men in various stages of fatherhood. A lot of them are rappers. For example, one conversation I remember having was with Fabolous in a suite at Madison Square Garden while interviewing him about his "Soul Tape" project. He told me about his touring routine. No matter what, no matter where he is in the world he has to be home in time to take his son to school in the morning. I asked what inspired this staple in his fatherhood, he simply told me he wants to be the father he never had. Some men can make the excuse that because they didn't have a father their child will also be 'fine" without one. But REAL MEN don't lie to themselves or their children. They step up and find a way.

Another one of my favorite convos was on the set of the new *YO! MTV Raps.* Between takes I sat next to world famous Director Chris Robinson and we talked about fathering an adult child. This is seldom spoken of but is very pivotal as the decisions we make as adults have a way bigger impact on our lives. Chris shared some wisdom on how he made his son earn his role in the family business and didn't just hand him the directors chair once he felt he was ready. The blessing that being in a position to take advantage of nepotism and position your child for success is an amazing feeling. However, you want to make sure once you put them in position that they can not only keep it but push it further than you can. That's what fatherhood is all about.

I can go on and on and tell story after story. You'll come across a lot in this book. I hope you find this book to be as valuable and inspiring as I have, and that it helps you on your journey as a father.

Sincerely,
Esteban Serrano

MESSAGE TO NEW FATHERS

To all you new fathers out there, welcome to the club. This is the hardest job you will ever have. It'll also be the most rewarding one. I want to prepare you for the road ahead. As much as this journey is about your child, it's even more about you.

If I had to describe fatherhood in one word it'd be, "mirror." Fatherhood puts a spotlight on all your shortcomings and flaws and forces you to face them. The only way you can truly become a great father is to become a great man. This means dealing with the parts of you that hold you back from being everything your kid needs.

My father used to alway say I raised him. It wasn't until I became a father myself that I understood him. What he meant was I forced him to grow up so that he could be his best for me.

When I started out on this path I was selfish, lazy and condescending (to name a few). But you can't be selfish when you're a father. You have to be selfless. You have to go from top priority to last place.

You can't be lazy because there is so much work to be done. I remember my wife telling me one day after I'd come home from work, "The people at your job get the best version of you and we get whatever's left." This rocked me to my core. She was right. When I came home, I was cooked. I was tired. I had nothing left to give. But my family didn't deserve that. They should get the best of me.

I couldn't be condescending to my children. That could crush their little spirits. I don't want to be a soul killer! I have to build them up!

This is HONESTLY the unspoken beauty of fatherhood. You will grow, mature and change for the better if you truly want to be the best dad you can be.

Lastly I want to leave you with this mantra. WHATEVER IS BEST FOR MY CHILD. This may be the most inconvenient and ego killing thing you live by but it will guarantee your child suffers the least they can at your hands. Live by that and you'll be great.

Congratulations. God bless you and your family.

MESSAGE TO STEP-FATHERS

To all you step-fathers out there, also welcome to the club. If God puts you in this position remember you are more than capable of fulfilling this role. I've been there and I know first hand how complicated and confusing it can be. But remember, ultimately, whatever's best for the child, wins.

In some cases your load as a step-father may be as simple as being another great example of a man. If that child's biological father is a willing and active participant, you may just need to be there for an occasional pat on the back or sounding board.

In other cases you may need to step all the way in, ten toes down. It's either you become their father or they won't have one.

In some cases it may be a balance of the two.

Whichever position you find yourself in, this book will help you navigate your fatherhood journey.

I was taught, if a child is in earshot of a man, that man is to look after that child. The fact that you opened this book and got this far shows you are that type of man and want to prepare yourself to be an active participant and not a bystander.

The world needs more men like you. Salute.

God bless you and your family.

THE INTRO

First and foremost let me address the legend in the room. The Notorious B.I.G. better known as Biggie is one of my favorite rappers. He was also an outspoken RAP DAD. In his breakout hit record Juicy he starts the record off, before he even spits a bar, by mentioning his daughter. Now I ain't gonna quote the lyric cause I ain't tryna get sued but you can pull it up and listen for yourself.

From jump B.I.G. let it be known that he's dedicating, and possibly even risking, his life to feeding his daughter. This is one of the many shining examples of how prominent a subject fatherhood has been and still is in Hip Hop culture.

In my experience as a father I've learned these ten Commandments both by succeeding and more importantly for you the reader by failing, learning my lessons and applying them moving forward. This book is inspired by the Notorious B.I.G.'s, Ten Crack Commandments and while that inspiration will be littered through the book it is not a verbatim, blatend interpretation. This is not a *step-by-step booklet*. Every father's journey is different just like every child is different. I have three sons. While they are very similar they could not be more different from each other regardless of them sharing DNA and growing up in the same environment. They are who they are and their individual personalities, love languages, styles of learning and retaining information make each of them unique and therefore my approach as a father has to be just as unique and tailored for my sons to receive the information, interpret it, apply it and thrive.

These Ten Dad Commandments are a foundation for great fatherhood. It is not the only source of information you will need. It should not be the only book or information you get along your journey. These commandments are to set you up to be a great father. As I mentioned in the Message to New Fathers, fatherhood is a mirror. Your child will show you flaws, weaknesses and shortcomings about yourself that you need to address in order to be the best version of yourself and therefore the best father you can be for your child. This is a humbling process. Leave your ego at the door. There is no room for selfishness. It's all about what's best for your child.

This is not the book you read under the impression that at the end you will know how to be a father and will have learned everything you need to teach your child. This book lays out the things you need to know and begin to apply so you are knowledgeable, prepared and in position to parent from a centered and powerful place.

To reference The Notorious B.I.G.'s, commandments, fatherhood is "*not for freshmen*." This is the big leagues gentleman. Let's approach it that way.

Chapter One

KNOW YOUR ROLE (WHAT IS A FATHER?)

I am a firm believer that you can not fulfill a role that you have not yet defined. So in order to be a great father you must first know what a father is. So first and foremost I want to help define "father."

I've asked a lot of RAP DADS and done a lot of research on this question, "What is a father?" The answers vary widely. Some say a king. Some say a provider. Some say a leader. Some say a role model. All are true in their own ways.

A father is responsible for providing emotional and financial support to his children and is often seen as a role model and authority figure in the family. In addition to providing for and nurturing his children, a father may also play a role in disciplining and guiding them as they grow and develop.

The presence of a father can have a significant impact on a child's development. Research has shown[1] that children who have a positive and supportive relationship with their fathers tend to have better outcomes in areas like academic achievement, social skills, and mental health. On the other hand, children who do not have a father figure or who have a negative relationship with their fathers may be at a disadvantage in these areas.

Far too often the role of a father gets whittled down to two symbols — a belt and a wallet. A father lays down the law and rules with an iron fist, characterized in most cases with a leather belt. Otherwise, the image of a father is of a worker who brings home the bacon and keeps the lights on. These are just the minimum, they are not the full scope of the role.

One of the least discussed and in my opinion, most important roles a father plays is giving emotional support to his children. We think of fathers as stone cold and mothers as a child's source of nurturing. However, A father can also play a vital role in providing emotional support to his children. This includes being available to listen, offer guidance and advice, and provide comfort and reassurance. Imagine what a well-rounded example of a man a child can get from a father who supports them in this way. That can not only be life changing but WORLD CHANGING as well.

Last and most important, a father is a spiritual guide. I am not a religious man. I am, however, a very spiritual being. Religion vs.Sp irituality is like the age-old argument of Rap vs. Hip-Hop. While they appear to be similar, the two are very different if you can recognize it. Anyway, I made sure I shared God with children. I didn't want to force a relationship on them but I wanted them to know he exists and to establish their own relationships. I share my spiritual journey with them and I am sure to point out the many ways God makes his presence felt in our daily lives. My spirituality is a huge part of my life. So you can't help but notice it if we hang out long enough. My kids notice it as well because of how I walk as a man of spirituality. As much as we laugh, joke, snap on each other and play around, they know I'm governed by a higher power and they know how big a role the law of karma plays in my life and theirs.

MY DEFINITION

For me, I define my role as a father as that of a servant king. Remember, the best and most successful kings throughout history are the ones who put their subjects first. They would do anything for them. They protected them. They provided for them. They made decisions with their subjects' best interests at heart. Not what's best for the king.

A father will play many roles in his life. You will be an Uber driver. You will be a chef. You'll be a coach. You'll be a referee. You get the point. But as long as you understand that you are to serve your child, you will fulfill every role with grace and dignity.

The "old-school" mentality of, "Daddy gets the big chair and big piece of chicken." is outdated. That approach will build resentment towards you and not foster love. It also sets the wrong example of what a father is. You don't want your kids to grow up and repeat that behavior.

There is nothing worse or more embarrassing than an entitled father. This is a man who thinks because he is the father things should go the way he says and everyone should bend to his will. If he doesn't wise up he'll see that approach blow up in his face.

You want to be a constant and consistent leader— a positive influence. This doesn't mean to be perfect; quite the opposite. Be honest and show grace when your kids make mistakes and own up to yours. That's what a real leader does. Too often our egos keep us from teaching our children valuable lessons about failure through our own examples. Truth be told, we are not always brave enough to admit we failed, but this is to the detriment of our children. I'll speak more on this in chapter eight.

Fathers are conveyors of moral values. They are pillars in the development of a child's emotional well-being, helping them to get to know themselves while they grow into their full potential.

CHOOSE YOUR STYLE

Now that we know what a father is, we should establish what kind of father you are or want to be. Remember the Wu-Tang Clan? They each had a very different and distinct style. There was the tiger style, drunken style, and we can't forget about the Wu-Tang sword style, but I digress. Parenting has many styles also.

Some of them you want to avoid. Like the "helicopter style." This is when you hover over your child. Smothering them so they don't have the space to grow into their own person. Then there's the "snowplow parent" also known as the lawnmower or bulldozer parent. This parent gets out in front of their child and removes all the obstacles in their way. You can imagine how bad this is for their children. If the first time your kid meets an obstacle is in college, you have failed!

The best in my opinion are the following, however keep in mind it really depends on the child:

-There's the " authoritative style" which is the fine balance of structure, discipline and rules with some wiggle room for grace and understanding.

-There's the "free-range style" which is letting your kid roam free and give them the space to get into trouble and learn from their decisions and mistakes. In this style, you take on more of an advisory role and help them decipher problems and scenarios that arise in their lives.

The truth of the matter is you want to take the MMA approach to parenting and learn all of them and apply them when the time is right.

When my kids were toddlers and tiny babies just learning to get around on their own I was a helicopter dad. When they entered elementary school and junior high school I was more of an authoritative dad. Then when they got to be high school and college age I became a free-range dad. I think it worked out best for my boys.

My father was definitely a free-range dad. I remember anytime I had a tough decision I'd go to him. He'd help me evaluate the pros and cons of my options and then leave it up to me to make the decision. This helped me think things through, weigh the consequences of my actions, and made me fully accountable for the decisions I made. I couldn't blame him or anyone else if things went wrong.

I GOT A STORY TO TELL...LOST BOY

I remember the day my son dropped the clue it was time for me to go from authoritative to free-range. He was in fourth or fifth grade. We were running late that morning and he'd missed the bus. But his school was only three or four blocks away from our house. So I told him to walk. He looked at me like I was sending him to the jungle. We lived in a suburban town where crime was literally zero!

He said, "I don't know how to get there on my own!" I looked back at him like he was the biggest fool on planet earth. I said, " you've been going to this school for two years now. Every day." He said, "I get driven on the bus. I don't pay attention to the directions." Then I got a lil testy and said, "Use your brain kid! Do you know how to get to the playground across the street from your school? The one where you have recess every day?"

He thought about it for a second. He realized he would go there by himself after school or on weekends to meet up with his friends. But it still didn't click for him. He said, "yeah I know how to get there," with a tone almost like, *what does that place have to do with anything?*

I said, "ok, so if you can get from here to the playground, can you get from the playground to school?" He thought for a second and said, "yeah." It was starting to make sense to him.

Then I said, "well, you know how to get to school then, huh?" The lightbulb went off and he excitedly said, yeah and rushed out the door. It's almost like he had tunnel vision and it hadn't occurred to him that there are many ways to solve a problem.

Once I realized he was a little paralyzed by his comfy routines, my wife and I threw a big challenge his way a few years later:

When he turned thirteen, he wanted to learn to DJ. So we put him in the Scratch Academy in The Village in Manhattan. When we signed him up, we explained to him we'd make the trip into the city and back home with him the first two times. Then he was on his own.

This introduced a host of potential issues and new responsibilities. He needed bus tickets and a metrocard for the subway ride for both legs of the trip. He also needed to make sure he got to the bus on time so he wouldn't be late for his class.

My wife and/or I took him round trip the first two times and then he was on his own. Everything went well the first couple trips after that. Then one evening, I got a call while I was at work. "Pop, I don't have enough money to get from class back to the bus stop that takes me home." I said, "Do you have any cash to put money on the metrocard?" He said "no." I asked him what block he was on. He told me, "8th & Broadway." I said, "Well I guess you are going to have to walk from 8th & Broadway to me at 32nd & 7th." He said, "You can't come get me?" I said, "No dude, I'm at work and it's your responsibility to make sure you have enough for travel. I'll see you when you get here." He said ok, hung up the phone, and about an hour or so later he met me at work.

The best part about that was it NEVER happened again. He learned the lesson and it stuck with him.

I say all that to say you must be willing to adapt your style to the needs of your child. When he was in high school and I went total free-range on him, he flourished. He knew his way in and out of the city. He knew how to navigate the New York City subway. He'd take his friends into the city all the time to explore, see concerts, shop and eat. He became an independent city kid. So when he moved all the way to Philadelphia for college it was easy for him to take public transportation wherever he needed to go because he had four to five years of experience navigating on his own.

THE IMPACT OF A FATHER'S ABSENCE

I'd be remiss if I didn't go into the impact fatherlessness can have on a child. Just as a father's presence can bring a wealth of nurturing benefits to a child's life, their absence can have a long-lasting, well-documented negative impact.

Studies across the board show that children who grew up without fathers are more likely to end up living below the poverty line, drop out of school, become addicted to drugs, or end up in prison. The impact of not having a father figure during childhood can be colossal. Today, growing up without a father is increasingly being likened to a trauma that children struggle with for the rest of their lives. It's a painful experience that can lead to feelings of low self-esteem, unworthiness and both identity, and self-love issues.

This reminds me of the iconic *Fresh Prince of Bel Air*[2] episode where Will's dad comes back after he'd all but grown up, just to leave him again. That was one of the most powerful scenes in my TV watching memory. No matter how cool Will was or how great his life was living in a mansion in Bel Air, he still wanted the acceptance of his father. His famous line before he collapsed into Uncle Phil's arms Will asked why, "he don't want me?"

(I'm not crying. You are. Back to the book.)

Shockingly, poor physical health is also linked to fatherlessness. With children growing up without fathers, they are more likely to suffer from acute and chronic health conditions throughout their lives, left literally and figuratively heartbroken. In addition, without a father figure to bond with in their developmental years, adults who've grown up without a father tend to struggle forming healthy attachments, hindering their chances of finding love or starting their own families.

One of my favorite songs on this topic is Kendrick Lamar's "Father Time."[3] The song really dives deep into how the term "daddy issues" is often referred to young ladies. While its impact on young men is often ignored but has a devastating impact. Be sure to check that out as your homework for this chapter. Just kidding…but listen though.

I GOT A STORY TO TELL…A$AP ROCKY LOVED HIS FATHER

While working for the music television network Fuse, I sat down to interview A$AP Rocky. I had a great relationship with Rocky because I was the first person to put him on TV. Soon after, we'd gone viral[4] for an interview I did with him at the South By Southwest (SXSW) music festival about his absence on XXL Magazine's "Freshman Class" list. My first time meeting Macklemore he said, "I know you, you're A$AP Rocky's personal interviewer." We all burst out laughing.

Anyways, the A$AP Rocky interview was conducted in December of 2012. Close to Christmas I decided, like I often did, to bring my youngest son to work with me. After our interview was done, Rocky met my son Mikael. He immediately started interacting with him. He asked him a bunch of questions: "Do you love your dad? Is he a cool dude? Does he play with you?" He then turned to me and said, "Make sure you take care of him. Treat him well." I was kind of taken aback. Rocky was low key grilling me but in a very loving way.

Later on that day, the talent rep from Fuse called to tell me that A$AP Rocky's father had passed away either that morning or the night before. The news put that moment into context. I find it amazing that artists are able to push through and still do the work in light of these incidents. But what that showed me was how much Rocky loved his father and for a moment, he saw his relationship reflected in that of my son and I.

Chapter Two

WATCH THE COMPANY YOU KEEP

'Watch the ones closest to you' is a common theme in Hip-Hop. In our favorite songs, movies, and books it always seems like the enemy is in the inner circle. Well, it ain't no different in fatherhood. It's time to cut the grass and watch the snakes run out of the garden.

Fatherhood is a great opportunity to both self-evaluate and evaluate the company you keep. A lot of times we keep people in our lives for different reasons. You've got your ride or die, day ones. You've got your party friends. You've got your sports friends, etc. But, you have to evaluate and intentionally decide who you're going to keep close and who you're going to let go once you hit the dad phase.

Fatherhood is a great excuse to purge unwanted or unwelcome people from your life. Your time is more valuable now than ever. You will feel it every minute you spend away from your child. That being said, use this new responsibility as an opportunity to let go of some people who don't add value to your life and therefore, won't add value to your child.

Now I'm not saying cut everybody off all together, I'm simply saying start to evaluate and categorize your friend group so you know who to prioritize with your precious time and who shouldn't get any.

You are going to want to build a community of great men around you for many reasons:

- **You'll need some advice.** Parenting is the Wild Wild West, especially in the beginning. So being able to call and lean on some folks who've been there before can be a blessing.

- **You'll need an escape.** When you are spending countless hours changing diapers, getting peed on (yes, this will happen), doing laundry and cleaning baby vomit, you'll need to detach. This is where some great friends can come into play. They can cheer you up, help you get a second wind, and toss you back into the ring.

- **To be great "play uncles."** For those unfamiliar with the concept of a "play uncle" this is someone who is like an uncle but is of no blood relation. My son's play uncles and godfathers were very well selected and are in many ways a group of like-minded men. They each are walking, talking, living reflections of the morals, values and spiritual ideals I possess and hold in high regard.

Not any and everyone should be allowed access to your child. These men are truly the only men to have that pass and it has paid tremendous dividends for not only me but my entire family. An added benefit of this process is you don't really notice how influenced you are by the company you keep but change the people you are around and a lot of things can change for you.

Have you ever heard the phrase "you are the sumtotal of the five people you spend the most time with?" The saying means that the people you spend the most time with can have a big influence on who you are as a person. It's like when you mix different colors together - each hue combines to create a new color that is a combination of all of them. In the same way, the people you spend the most time with can influence your thoughts, feelings, and behaviors. They can help shape your personality and the way you see the world. So, it's important to choose the people you spend time with wisely – because they can have a big impact on your life.

For example, if you spend a lot of time with kind and caring people, you might start to become more kind and caring yourself. But if you spend a lot of time with mean or selfish people, you might start to develop the same traits.. That's why it's important to surround yourself with good people who help bring out the best in you.

ACQUAINTANCES

There's always that friend or play cousin who thinks he's teaching your kid to be tough when they "play fight." That same person may think it's funny to give your kids advice on the opposite sex. You and I know he is not to be taken seriously, but does your kid know that? If your child is introduced to someone through you, chances are they'll trust that person. One way to combat the bad ideas from taking root is to limit the access unworthy people have to your children.

Another course of action, if your child is old enough, is to tell your kids the truth about that person. "Don't listen to anything uncle 'Blah Blah' tells you- he's just playing around." If you don't make it clear, you'll leave room for interpretation and that ain't always good.

When I was growing up there were a bunch of men in my "village." Uncles on both sides of the family as well as my Pop's friends. I must say, I was surrounded by some stand-up men. To this day my uncles, real and pretend, are still part of my life. I make sure the same is true for my sons. The only men who have real access to them are a chosen few. My day one, tried and true friends. It's interesting to see how they are with my sons. They don't hesitate to love, teach and if needed, correct them. The majority of them don't even have kids of their own. It's just the nature of real men when they get around kids.

I also make sure I only hang with like minded individuals. So I'm not too concerned about my sons picking up unwanted habits from my homies because we are all in lock step.

One of the best parts of having a dope tribe of friends is they'll check you on things you are doing wrong or things you've mishandled in your parenting. Because I have the relationship I have with my crew, and because I don't have an ego when it comes to being a father, I learn from their perspectives. It's naive to think your way is best. Sometimes you need that fresh perspective to keep you on task. And the task at hand is being the best father you can be.

CHEATCODE

A great way to help your children discern for themselves is to point out the subtle differences between how certain people behave and how men in your tribe behave. This is an informative exercise for when you are spending time around people who are not in your circle. Examples include places like the barbershop, public transportation or shopping. I use these moments to show my kids, in a safe way, that not all men are like me and my crew. Knowing how to recognize the difference and then knowing how to interact with different people is something they will carry for life.

I remember my middle son, my clone, wasn't hanging out with the kids he grew up with during his late middle school and early high school years. When I asked him why he didn't hang with those kids anymore, he told me it was because they were into dumb stuff that he didn't want any part of. They'd do stupid kid stuff like cause trouble at the mall or sneak out the house late at night. My son, on his own, made the decision to separate himself from that element and it served him well. Whenever he did hang with kids from that crowd it was usually one or two and always on his terms.

It's worth mentioning my sons don't need external validation or to be part of the "it crowd" because of how they were raised. More on that in the next chapter. A big part of the village approach is that your village can also create a space where your children feel seen, accepted, appreciated and championed. When they know what real love feels like, no artificial or digital like or comment can take its place.

Chapter Three
PROTECT

In this chapter I ain't about to tell you to go out and buy a gun, unless you've got daughters, JUST KIDDING! The "protection" I'm referring to includes, but goes beyond, their physical well being. As fathers, it's our responsibility to protect our children from harm and to provide a safe, nurturing environment for them to grow and develop. This can include protecting them from physical dangers, such as accidents or injuries, as well as protecting them from emotional and psychological harm.

Some specific ways we can protect our children include the following:

1. **Ensuring that our homes are safe and secure, with appropriate safety measures in place such as smoke detectors and childproofing** The childproofing phase is most definitely the most annoying and inconvenient of times but it is short lived and well worth it.

2. **Teaching them about safety rules and procedures, such as looking both ways before crossing the street or wearing a helmet while riding a bike** Another very underrated safety rule is dressing weather appropriately. Too often I see kids wearing ball shorts and crocs year around in places where there's four seasons. It's a real cultural epidemic of casual wear. I've gotten so many compliments from teachers and neighbors about how well dressed my children are for the weather. When it rains they have rain boots or sneakers that are waterproof. When it snows they have snow boots, hats, gloves, scarves etc. This not only falls under safety but also teaches them to plan ahead and be prepared.

3. **Monitoring their online activity and helping them to understand the risks and dangers of the internet, such as cyberbullying and online predators** I'm not by any means a cyber stalker with my kids. I don't have parental blocks on them at all. I grew up with parents in their twenties and they never censored me and I don't censor my children. This is a very unpopular position but it most definitely works for me and my family.

That being said, I also don't ignore the dangers of life online. When my kids started playing C.O.D. (Call of Duty) and would be in matches with other kids and even adults who would be using racial slurs and insane foul language. It was a great talking point/teachable moment for our family.

Another HUGE topic was sexting. I heard about a neighbor of mine who got hit with child pornography charges because his daughter was caught up in some underaged revenge porn. Turns out she went through her boyfriend's phone, found a nude photo another girl sent him, sent it to herself and then blasted it out to the entire school. The girl in the photo was underaged. So because of that, coupled with the fact the device was registered to the father, he got hit with the charges. That is some LIFE RUINING stuff. This too became a topic of discussion around the dinner table in my house.

Instead of sheltering my children from the real world I decided to walk it with them and prepare them for it. That way, once they leave my supervision, they are familiar with these things and know how to act. Again, this is not a popular stance on how to deal with this type of subject matter but this is how I roll. There's no judgment if you disagree - you do whatever you think is best.

A big part of why I believe my children are not easily influenced or hooked on social media is because of the attention they've gotten from my wife and I. Studies show[5] that a real life hug and a "like" on a social media post release the same amount of dopamine in your brain. Dopamine is a chemical released in the brain that makes you feel good. Humans, especially children, are constantly seeking attention and validation. If they don't get it from us they'll seek it out. It's best to be their source.

1. **Providing guidance and support to help them make healthy and safe choices, such as avoiding risky behaviors like drug use or unprotected sex** Let me also say, if you think you know the right time to have the talk about

the birds and the bees (aka sex), move it up a couple years. These kids are ADVANCED nowadays! I missed the window on my middle son by a year and he was active in these streets! Better to be early than late. Take it from me.

2. **Modeling healthy behavior and communication, and setting appropriate boundaries and expectations for their behavior** Our consistency becomes their security.

3. **Protecting them from emotional abuse or neglect, whether it is within the family or from outside sources** Emotional abuse is sometimes hard to recognize. Especially considering that we may be the abusers and not even know it. That's why it's so important to check yourself and allow others to be able to check you. I remember I was verbally disciplining my son in public and I was going a little too far. I'd asked him a question a few times and he was distracted and not listening. He was just being a kid doing what kids do. But I was frustrated. I said something about not understanding how he couldn't hear me with his big ole ears. He quickly grabbed his ears and was hurt by what I said to him. Once I realized it I snapped back to reality, checked myself and apologized.

Unfortunately, children could be abused by close family friends or even loved ones. Oftentimes they may not be willing to tell you because of the shame or fear for their safety. This is why you want to constantly be checking in on them and be conscious of their state of being around certain places or people.

Some signs a child could be suffering from emotional abuse are:

1. Extreme changes in behavior, such as becoming very clingy or withdrawing from social interaction

2. Sudden changes in school performance or difficulty concentrating

3. Expressions of worthlessness or self-hatred

4. Excessive fear or anxiety, particularly around a particular person or situation

5. Difficulty trusting others or forming relationships

6. Physical symptoms such as stomach aches, headaches, or sleep problems that cannot be explained by a medical condition

By being a proactive and protective father, you can help your children feel safe, supported, and loved, which is essential for their physical, emotional, and psychological well-being.

PROTECT THEIR PEACE

This may sound "spiritual" or "esoteric" but this is basic. If you can get this to take root in your child when they are young, they will be unshakable as adults.

It's unfortunate but a lot of adults don't know how important protecting your peace is. Once you learn that happiness is a choice and only YOU can make YOURSELF happy, it's a game changer. You'll never run around looking for someone or, God forbid, something to be your source of happiness. Knowing you are the source means no one else can make you happy and more importantly no one else can steal your joy.

Teaching our children to be aware of their state of being from moment to moment is the beginning of teaching them to protect their peace. They first need to be able to recognize their own state. Ask them how they feel periodically. Let that spark a conversation. Ask a few follow up questions like, "Why do you feel that way?" or "What made you feel like this?" Then, help them understand that they are in control of their happiness.

You can almost gamify it for them. Pretend you are soldiers and we must protect our peace to ensure victory. "Who's trying to steal our peace? Is it a messy room? Is it homework? Is it a friend? Let's take them out. We must protect our peace. No one can take it from us!"

Here are some ways we as fathers can help protect our child's peace and promote a sense of calm and well-being:

1. **Set boundaries and establish routines** Setting clear boundaries and establishing routines can help children feel more secure and provide a sense of structure and pre-dictability in their lives. This might include setting limits on screen time, establishing bedtimes, and setting rules for behavior.

2. **Practice mindfulness and self-regulation** Teaching chil-dren mindfulness and self-regulation techniques such as deep breathing, progressive muscle relaxation, and visu-

alization, can help them manage their emotions and reactions and promote a sense of inner peace.

3. **Encourage healthy habits** Helping children develop healthy habits such as regular exercise, a healthy diet, and sufficient sleep, can promote physical and emotional well-being and contribute to a sense of peace and balance.

4. **Promote open and honest communication** Encourage open and honest communication with your children and model good communication skills yourself. This can help them feel more connected to you and create a safe and supportive environment for them to share their thoughts and feelings.

5. **Spend quality time together** Make time to connect with your children and engage in activities that are relaxing and enjoyable for everyone. This can help build a strong and positive relationship and contribute to a sense of peace and well-being.

6. **Seek help when needed** If your child is experiencing significant stress or distress, it is important to seek help from a mental health professional or other reputable literature to address their needs and promote their overall well-being.

PROTECT THEIR SELF CONFIDENCE

Self-confidence is an important quality for children to develop, as it can influence their emotional well-being, social interactions, and overall sense of self-worth. When you know who you are NO ONE can convince you otherwise.

My sons are so self confident they won't even let ME convince them they are corny! My son was about seven years old when he got up the courage to storm into the living room and boldly voice his decision to go to LEGO camp. He walked up on me, got right in my face and said, "Pop, I know you won't like this, but I *want* to go to LEGO camp." I don't know why he even thought I would put up a fight with him. I love playing LEGO with him. This was too great a moment for me to put out his fire, so I just shut up and listened. He continued, "I know there's one nearby that's starting soon and I want to go." I said, "Ok, I'm down to take you to LEGO camp but I'm telling you right now, when you commit to this camp, you are going to go to every single class." He looked at me like I was crazy. I continued, "LEGO camp ain't just a bunch of kids playing LEGO, it's all about robotics, engineering and computer science. So be prepared."

I drove him to this expensive LEGO camp. On our way he was so excited. I dropped him off and he ran into the building on his own. When I went to pick him up he looked defeated. I asked him how it went and he said, almost reluctantly, "You were right. It was all about pulleys and levers and science. We didn't even get to build much." I tried my best not to react much. I just said, "We'll see how tomorrow goes."

I was so proud of him for overcoming his fear of my reaction and speaking up for himself and what he wanted. I'm not a "yes dad." If I don't like something, even if my kid is into it, I let them know it's not for me. That doesn't mean that I won't support them in it, it just means that I don't like it personally. The gift and the curse of keeping it real with your kids is they can misunderstand you not liking something personally and misinterpret it as you not liking it for them as well. We are talking about children here- their brains are not fully developed yet so I get it. Although I love LEGO, I don't know where this came from.

My wife and I went out of our way to build up their self-confidence. We knew how important it would be to their futures. My wife would have these affirmations for my sons. She called them "I am's." She would have them repeat it out loud to her. She would have them on three-by-five cards all over the house and on the mirrors in every room. They'd say things like, *I am smart. I am creative. I am handsome.* I highly suggest you employ this with your children.

Another proud dad moment came at the dinner table one day. My middle son had just picked up the guitar about a month prior to this conversation. We are all at the table and he's talking about building some sick guitar that combines a rhythm guitar and a bass guitar on one instrument. My oldest son said, "You just started playing guitar. You can't build one." My middle son put his foot down at the table and said, "Don't tell me what I can't do!" We all, including my oldest, applauded him for taking that stance. Again, once you have self-confidence, you are unshakeable. No matter who is trying to convince you – you won't budge.

Here are a few ways fathers can help protect and nurture a child's self-confidence:

1. **Encourage self-expression and independence** Encourage your child to express their thoughts, feelings, and ideas. Give them the opportunity to make decisions and take on age-appropriate responsibilities. This can help them develop self-confidence and a sense of autonomy.

2. **Provide positive reinforcement** Praise your child for their efforts, successes, and positive behaviors, rather than focusing solely on their mistakes or failures. This can help boost their self-confidence and self-esteem.

3. **Help them develop skills and interests** Encourage your child to pursue their interests and hobbies Help them develop skills and competencies in areas that they enjoy. This can help them feel confident and capable in their abilities.

4. **Be a supportive and caring role model** Show your child love and support, and model healthy behaviors and attitudes. This can help them feel valued and supported, which can boost their self-confidence and self-esteem.

5. **Seek help when needed** If your child is experiencing significant self-doubt or low self-esteem, it is important to seek help from a mental health professional or other research material to address their needs and promote their overall well-being.

PROTECT THEIR CREATIVITY

I'm a creative by nature and by trade. I'm a television producer. My wife is also a creative. She's an author and entrepreneur. So fostering our children's creativity was top of our list. I remember one day asking my wife when her childlike imagination died. Without hesitation she said when adults put limitations on my ideas or told me to think realistically. From that day on we vowed never to do that to our kids and to never allow anyone else to do that to them.

That's how you get a rap group made up of a thirteen, ten and seven-year-old performing a song they wrote and produced live on MTV. That's right. My kids wrote a viral hit song about their favorite tv show *Stranger Things* and it went so crazy it landed them a performance spot on live TV. When you create the environment, nurture their interests, and support them as much as you can –watch them fly!

Creativity is an important quality for children to develop, as it can foster problem-solving skills, critical thinking, and self-expression.

Here are a few ways that a father can help protect and nurture a child's creativity:

1. **Encourage exploration and experimentation** Encourage your child to try new things, experiment with different materials and techniques, and express their ideas and thoughts through art, writing, music, or other creative outlets.

2. **Provide a supportive and open-minded environment** Create a supportive and open-minded environment that encourages creativity, allowing your child the freedom to explore and express themselves.

3. **Foster a growth mindset** Encourage your child to embrace challenges and setbacks as opportunities for growth and learning, rather than viewing them as failures. This can help them feel more confident in their abilities and be open to trying new things.

4. **Expose them to a wide range of experiences** Provide your child with a wide range of experiences and expose them to different cultures, art forms, and ideas. This can help stimulate their creativity and inspire them to think in new and innovative ways.

5. **Encourage problem-solving** Encourage your child to think creatively and approach problems in unique and innovative ways. This can help them develop their critical thinking skills and feel more confident in their ability to solve problems.

6. **Seek out opportunities for creative expression** Look for opportunities for your child to express their creativity through activities such as art, music, or theater, or through more everyday activities such as cooking or building.

BE A RIDE OR DIE DAD

One of the craziest things my dad would say to me was, "I'd do anything for you. If you want to rob a bank, I'd do it with you." He'd also say, "If you're going to drink or try any drugs it better be with me. I'd be so upset if you smoked your first joint with someone else." This crazy talk was genius. Essentially what he did was prove how *ride or die* he was for me and opened a strong line of communication about things that you'd never talk to your parents about. This is another way he was protecting me. By volunteering to be my co-defendant, he was ensuring he'd be involved in my crazy plans. By expressing how disappointed he'd be if I drank or smoked for the first time without him, he was not only normalizing the use of drugs and alcohol but he was once again volunteering to be there to monitor and protect me.

I'm not gonna sit here and lie to you and say this will 100% guarantee that your kid will tell you EVERYTHING. 'Cause it won't! However it sets a foundation that you can continue to reinforce throughout your child's life. For example…

One morning my oldest son, a sophomore in high school at the time, woke up early for school. He got fully dressed and rushed out the door at 6:30 in the morning. This was quite unusual because this kid needed multiple alarms and in person attempts to wake up on a school day. His mother, wide awake in the living room, noticed him heading towards the door. She asked him where he was off to so early. He thought about it for a second and then said, "I'm going to the corner store for a snack." Now, again, it's 6:30 am and the corner store in our neighborhood didn't open until 8:00 am. After my wife informed him he then replied, "Oh, I'll go to the liquor store then." The liquor store doesn't open until noon. After a few attempts he finally confessed to his mother that he was going to meet a friend on the corner to give him some of his *urine*.

His friend was caught using drugs. Since then, he had been randomly drug tested by his parents. Clearly the kid was not clean and therefore asked my son to help him out.

My wife came into our bedroom to wake me up and fill me in on what was going on. I, without a pause, asked my son, "How are you going to do the exchange? Urine has to be kept at a body temperature in order to pass the test. If it drops lower than ninety-seven degrees, it will trigger a failed test."

He was shocked – not only because we weren't upset with him, but because we were trying to help him. I was happy he had clean piss! You'd think this would really solidify the fact we have his back and we'll do anything for him if included...but it didn't.

So the first time he smoked weed and got so high he couldn't move I drove to the house he was at, picked him up and brought him home no questions asked. My wife tended to him to make sure he was ok. It was this time he finally got the point that we were ride or die.

When he went away for the weekend after prom and got drunk, his girlfriend called us to help him. My wife told him to eat and get good sleep and it'll be fine in the morning, to which it was. The fact he called us in his time of need knowing we wouldn't judge or scold him but support and love him meant the world to us.

Keep your cool and remember the plan is to gain and keep their trust. Ask yourself what's more important: that you scold your children and drive a wedge between each other OR keeping the lines of communication flowing so you are always in the loop?

This reminds me of another genius teachable moment I learned from my father. My sister, who was a senior in high school at the time, was in the backyard at our family barbeque. My dad poured her a sangria. I asked him why he was allowing her to drink. He said, "Next year she'll be in college and I don't want her first experiences drinking to be by herself. I want her to learn her tolerance and limits while I can watch her." Not many of us would have the foresight to think about doing this. How many people do you know go off to college and get trashed and have really bad things happen as a result? This too is a form of protection: Proactive protection.

Chapter Four

ACTION! GET INVOLVED

I f you are reading this book, chances are you are or want to be an active, involved father. Salute to you. There's nothing more inspiring, encouraging and important to a child than a father who will get down on his hands and knees and play, read, pray etc. with them.

What you are doing for your child is creating a positive impression on them on many levels. As an example of a man, you are showing them that nothing is beneath you. You're also showing them that you are willing to leave your comfort zone and be vulnerable with them. Your children are allowed to lead you and teach you things about their interests. This will impact your sons as an amazing point of reference when they become men. It'll also impact your daughters when choosing a boyfriend or spouse. These times are very precious and impressionable.

When you're an active father you are supporting your child's development by helping support their physical, emotional, and psychological development. By spending time with your child, offering guidance and support, and being a positive role model, you can help your child grow and thrive. You are also building a strong, positive relationship with them which can have lasting benefits for their well-being and sense of self-worth. Research[6] has shown that children with Involved fathers tend to have better outcomes in terms of academic achievement, social and emotional development, and overall well-being. As an added bonus, being an active father can also be beneficial for your own well-being, as it can provide a sense of purpose and fulfillment and enhance your life.

SHOW THEM HOW DEDICATED YOU ARE EVEN WITH THINGS YOU'RE NOT INTERESTED IN

I'm not going to lie. I failed HARD at this one. My son was head over heels into the video game, *Minecraft*. One morning, while eating breakfast, He lost his mind at the sighting of a Spider Jockey. That is a very rare thing to see in the game. He was so excited he could barely speak. He said, "Pop look! Oh my God! A Spider Jockey! Super rare! Super rare!" I looked down my nose at this kid with a disgust that completely crushed his moment. He kinda snapped back to reality and the thrill was gone. I felt like crap. I was so disappointed in myself for stealing his joy. I vowed then and there to never let that happen again.

The next thing he was really into was a toy called *Beyblade*. I bought him a stadium and a bunch of stuff he could play with. I even played with him so he knew I was down.

I told you, the craziest part of fatherhood is the mirror. You get to see yourself in a whole new light. If you are paying attention, you will become a better man.

I GOT A STORY TO TELL...GANGSTERS MAKE THE BEST FATHERS PT. ONE

During my time working with Atlantic Records, I went to rapper Maino's house to film him as he got a huge tattoo on his stomach. Now Maino has an infamous reputation from his days in the street. He served jail time for a drug related kidnapping and he has a big scar on his face from an altercation. He called that his good side whenever I'd film him. The tattoo was to commemorate his five to fifteen-year prison sentence. He explained to me that he could have gotten out of prison in five years with good behavior but didn't, implying he was not well behaved while locked up. This was just to paint a picture of the type of guy we knew him to be.

While spending the day with him and his tattoo artist, he got on the phone with his son. I could obviously hear their conversation. At one point Maino asked his son about his homework. He then went on to remind his son to put his completed homework in a particular colored folder. If he didn't, the teacher would not know it was completed and he would not get credit for it. This is a great example of an active father. I'm not aware of his relationship with the mother of his son. I wasn't aware of the custody or what have you. But, I do know that Maino made sure his son was supported. This child knew that his father was looking out for him, no matter where he was in the world.

BE THEIR NUMBER ONE FAN

There's nothing like the support of a father. I remember growing up I wanted to be in Hip-Hop so badly. I knew I had to be part of the culture. At the time the only way I knew how to get involved was to become a rapper. One Christmas I'd asked my parents for a karaoke machine. It had two tape decks and a microphone so I could play instrumentals on one deck and record my vocals over the beat on a tape in the other deck. My dad was very curious about this request. He'd always wanted me to play basketball. Growing up, that was his passion. I had a natural talent for it but it wasn't my passion.

My parents got me the machine and I went in! Eventually my mom and dad asked me to record a demo for them. They wanted to hear the kind of music I was making and that would determine how involved they'd be in my passion. This was genius but at the same time very intimidating. I put together a few songs and gave them the tape. They hopped in the car and rode around listening to it. I stayed home and hid in my room.

Now, my father is the original RAP DAD. He got me into Hip-Hop so I know he knew his stuff. He was a passionate and opinionated listener. He wasn't one of those, "I just like the beats" type of Rap fans. He listened to N.W.A, Public Enemy, Wu-Tang Clan and Rakim. He was about the lyrics.

My parents came back and called me down to the living room. They were impressed. I had their full support. The next week or so my dad bought me an MPC 200XL. That's an iconic beat machine. It was a lot of money at the time too. That was a real investment.

Something similar happened with my clone Esteban. When he was about seven years old, I took him to a concert. This was fresh on the heels of his very first music festival experience at Lollapalooza in Chicago.

Anyway, after about three songs, he was ready to go. On the way home I asked him why he wanted to leave. "'Cause I can do better than that," he replied. "Oh word!?!" I inquisitively smirked. That night, when we got home, I pulled up some instrumentals and challenged him to write his first song. He killed it. He was a natural.

His song had a message. It had melody and flow. He even had adlibs. My mind was blown. I knew he'd be the best rapper of all time. Eventually he joined forces with his brothers. The three of them became the TRNDSTTRS (trendsetters without the vowels). They released a few songs and videos on YouTube. They even got to perform live on MTV. They killed that too. During that performance they were jumping on the couches and high fiving the crowd. Pull it up on YouTube. It's dope.

Eventually they stopped making Rap music and discovered the guitar. Now, they are a Rock band called Cold Court. Don't ask me to describe their sound because I wouldn't know how to begin. I'm at every show filming their sets.  Actually, for their first ever show as a band my wife and I wore t-shirts with their baby pictures on the front. It started as a joke about how committed we were to being fans. My wife took it literally and the boys thought it was adorable.

I look at their interests not only as an opportunity for them to explore, learn and develop some skills, look at it in the same way for you. Nurturing their talents is a great way to strengthen the bond between you and your kids. But, know your role. Don't be a trophy dad. Don't be one of the guys cursing at the coach and ref and getting kicked out of the gym.

You are the hype man. You are not the star. Whatever your kid wants to do, you are there to support. If they change directions, be there to help them chart the new path. It's about their journey. Let them live their life. Don't get in the way.

DON'T BE AN ABSENT FATHER, BUT PHYSICALLY PRESENT, FATHER

This is another one I struggled with early on in my fatherhood journey. I was there. I wasn't all that involved. My excuse was, when they get older I'll hang with them and play catch etc. Thank God my wife was excellent at speaking to me in a way that challenged me for the better. She showed me opportunities where I could be present and involved, even when they were young. I eventually got it. Thank God I did because the damage of being in the house but disengaged is severe.

Here are a few ways you can be an absent father while living in the same house as your child:

1. Neglecting your responsibilities as a parent, such as providing for your child's physical and emotional needs, can make you an absent father, even if you are physically present in the same house.

2. Being emotionally distant or uninvolved in your child's life can also make you an absent father. This might involve not showing interest in your child's life, not responding to their emotional needs, or not being available for support and guidance.

3. Spending a significant amount of time away from home

or engaging in activities that do not involve your child can also make you an absent father. This might include working long hours, traveling frequently, or engaging in hobbies or interests that do not involve your child.

4. Failing to communicate with your child or not being present and engaged when you are with them can also make you an absent father. This might involve ignoring your child when they are talking to you, not making an effort to spend quality time with them, or not being responsive to their needs and wants.

YOU WILL REGRET NOT BEING INVOLVED

The last thing you want as a father is to live with regret. In this role, if you regret not being involved, it could have life altering consequences. This is one of those times you want to employ all the sports pep talks and cliches you've heard throughout your life:

"Leave it all out on the field."
"Give 110%!"
"Play every play like it's fourth and inches."
"You miss 100% of the shots you don't take."

This time around it's all true! Take it from a dad with three teenagers, time flies. Right now you're changing diapers and next thing you know you're dropping your kid off at college. We don't have the luxury of time. Take advantage of the time you have and be present in the moment. Do what you say you're going to do and always remember, "WHATEVER IS BEST FOR MY CHILD, WINS!"

Chapter Five

LOVE, EMPATHY & COMPASSION

This chapter will be broken into a few parts. This is the critical, secret ingredient to making an amazing human being. We can talk about protection, safety, security, education and all that, but at the end of the day, our job as fathers is to add a great human being into the world.

HONOR THY WIFE (OR BABY MOM)

Let's start at the foundation. This has a huge impact on your children whether you realize it or not. MOST children learn by observation. Since the family is the first social group kids come in contact with, it's vital that a good impression is made. This could impact how your sons treat women (including their own mothers). It could also influence what type of partner your daughters choose. It could set the wrong example of how to communicate love and cause a lot of pain and childhood trauma.

For some this might be a sensitive subject, but a highly important one nonetheless. Our children learn a lot from our words but more from our behavior. Our children don't see our intentions or our circumstances. They are too young to grasp the full scope of what's going on around them. At the same time they are highly impressionable. This is why it's so important to show them how a man conducts himself with a woman.

This is especially important, if your baby's mother isn't very respectful of you around your child. You should show your child how a man conducts himself in this situation. Again, actions speak louder than words, but words coupled with actions sends a clear message to your child. Someone needs to set a positive example and be the "bigger person." Why not you dad?

I GOT A STORY TO TELL...FOCUSED FATHER

I remember a time I saw an irate mother screaming at a father about child support. The mother was berating this man, not only out in public but in front of his daughter. The woman yelled, "I don't need your money." The father yelled back. "You think I give you this money, for you? No! I give it to you for her. Because I'm taking care of my child." I remember thinking to myself, that's a man right there. His baby mom is out in the streets yelling at him and telling him she doesn't need his money and instead of being selfish and egotistical he let her and his daughter know who he is and what he stood for. Do you know how many guys would have put their money back in their pockets and left? Not anyone reading this book obviously.

When all else fails remember this: *When worst comes to worst, my child comes first.* As long as you keep that in mind and take that to heart you will not lose to your ego in tough moments.

For the Girl Dads, this will be a very important lesson for your daughters. We hope to leave an impression on our little girls that make them want a guy like their daddy. This could also backfire and set the wrong example of "acceptable behavior." Later on, your daughter could end up with a guy who speaks to her like you speak to her mother, thinking it's ok. In an extreme case, she could even think it's a sign of real love and look for a verbally abusive partner because that's how daddy talks.

As children get older, hormones start to kick in and they start to test boundaries. They don't want to be looked at as little kids anymore but are not yet young adults. This is also a crucial time to reinforce that example. When I was at this age, my mother would often express feeling disrespected because I took my sweet time to do the things she'd ask of me. My father sat me down and painted my mother in a new light for me. He said, "Listen man. That's your mom…but that's my woman! You should not be disrespecting your mother, and as a man, I can not let you disrespect my woman. So get it together."

To use that same approach in a different way, I'll say this. To you, she's your lady or your baby's mother. To your child, she's their mother. She's the center of their world. We know how special moms are. Imagine the confusion, turmoil or trauma you can cause a child by belittling or disrespecting their world. This is why you have to be mindful of how you conduct yourself.

BONUS

Growing up in West Philadelphia during the crack epidemic, it was super important that my parents created a bubble of protection around me. I grew up a lot like the theme of Kendrick Lamar's *Good Kid, M.A.A.D City*[7] album captured. I was in the hood, but not *of* the hood. My father and many of the men I was surrounded by, stood in stark contrast to the males I would come in contact with throughout my life. It taught me that being different was not only ok but expected. That had a rippling effect on my self esteem and pride. I didn't feel the need to "fit in" because my understanding and expectation was that I was supposed to be different.

Seeing the men in my life interact with their friends, neighbors etc. taught me that being different didn't mean alienating the rest of society. It taught me to have compassion and empathy in my relationships with others. One of the biggest examples was my god-father, Uncle Harry. His best friend growing up had gotten into drugs and was clearly never the same. My uncle never turned his back on his friend. He didn't treat him like less of a man. Instead he loved him and treated him like he always had. This humanized people battling with substance abuse for me. This taught me that they are not to be cast aside but instead they needed to be loved and included.

ACTIONABLE STEP

Remember, the fatherhood journey is filled with just as many teachable moments for your child as it is for you. Our kids are a reflection of us. They have our DNA and therefore our gifts and our flaws could be passed on to them. How you conduct yourself in the presence of your child will communicate a lot not only to them but to you if you are conscious. Are you patient or are you quick to anger? Do you have strong self-control or do you allow others to take you off your square? Do you defuse a situation or are you fanning the flame? Pay close attention to your behavior and evaluate the harmful behaviors you don't want to pass on to your kids. They deserve the best version of you, and you want to be the best version of yourself for them. That's why you are reading this book.

LOVE

This four letter word is everything. It is the end all be all when it comes to fatherhood. There are many different kinds of love. Each is equally important and all are needed to make a well rounded member of society.

AFFECTIONATE LOVE - This is the love that is expressed through physical touch, such as hugs, kisses, and holding hands. Affection is important to a child's development because it helps to build a sense of trust and security, which is essential for healthy emotional and psychological growth. Affectionate interactions, such as physical touch, positive verbal exchanges, and responsive attention, help children feel safe and valued, which in turn allows them to explore their environment and develop new skills.

Affectionate interactions can also help to regulate children's emotions and behavior, and can serve as a buffer against stress and negative experiences. I read that just holding hands[8] with someone can have a number of positive effects on the human body, both physically and emotionally. Physically, it can lower blood pressure and heart rate, as well as release oxytocin, a hormone associated with bonding and trust. Emotionally, holding hands can reduce stress and anxiety.

When I was a little boy my dad would kiss me on the forehead and on the cheek. He had a prickly beard and I hated it. He told me that on my wedding day he'd run up and kiss me on the lips right in front of everyone. He was joking. That experience made me think I'd never kiss my sons. But when they were babies I couldn't help but kiss their lil' faces off!

Quick side-story. My little sister hated my dad's beard too. One day he came home and tried to kiss her and she told him she hated his beard. Don't you know this man went and shaved it off immediately? And then she still wouldn't kiss him. Little girls have that effect on fathers.

Anyway, if you feel a little awkward about giving your kids affection, GET OVER IT. I guarantee you when they come up to hug you, or lay on you on the couch, or put their arm around you while hanging out, you are going to love it. Also, now that you know how beneficial it is, you should be even more convinced.

Some men think they should play rough with their kids. This too is a form of affection. But this should not be the ONLY form you show. Overall, affection plays a crucial role in shaping a child's sense of self and the way they interact with the world around them. So snuggle up dad!

SUPPORTIVE LOVE - This is the love that is expressed by being there for your child, both emotionally, practically, and helping them through difficult times. These times include times they've made mistakes. I think it's even more crucial to show supportive love when they mess up than any other time it applies.

Supportive love is important to a child's development because it helps to provide a sense of security, validation and encouragement. Children who feel supported and encouraged are more likely to develop a sense of self-efficacy, which can help them to explore their environment, develop new skills, and take healthy risks. Supportive love can be shown through positive reinforcement, validation of feelings, and encouragement of independence.

When children feel supported and encouraged, they are more likely to feel confident in expressing themselves and trying new things. Supportive love also helps children to develop a sense of self-esteem, self-worth and self-concept. It also helps children to be more resilient in the face of adversity and life challenges.

Furthermore, supportive love plays a crucial role in children's learning and academic development. Children who feel supported and encouraged are more likely to have positive attitudes towards learning, have higher levels of motivation, and perform better academically. Supportive love also helps children to cope with the challenges of growing up and navigate the world around them.

EMOTIONAL LOVE - This is the love that is expressed through feelings and sentiments, such as showing empathy and understanding towards your child's emotions.

Emotional love is important to a child's development because it helps to foster a sense of emotional well-being and self-worth. Children who feel emotionally loved and understood are more likely to develop healthy emotional regulation, which allows them to effectively manage their emotions and behavior. Emotional love can be shown through responsive and sensitive caregiving, active listening, and understanding of your child's emotions and needs.

Overall, emotional love plays a crucial role in shaping a child's emotional and psychological development, and in helping them to form healthy relationships and navigate the world around them.

If you are too rigid and have a skewed perception of masculinity that keeps you from showing emotional love or affection, you could be doing a lot of damage. To add to that, if your perception of masculinity causes you to force your children to "suck it up" and suppress their emotions that too can be dangerous. Emotions are a very real part of life. The "man up" or "boys don't cry" narrative is not only NOT TRUE, it paints a very toxic picture to our children.

TEACHING LOVE - This is the love that is expressed by passing on knowledge and values to your child, and guiding them through life's lessons.

Teaching love is important to a child's development because it helps children to learn and understand love in different forms, such as affection, protection, empathy and generosity. When children are taught about love and how to express it, they learn to understand and value the feelings and needs of others, which can help them to form healthy relationships.

When children are taught how to give and receive love, they learn to appreciate the importance of healthy relationships and the value of connecting with others. I'm sure you know some adults who either struggle with giving love or receiving it. Giving the teaching love early is the antidote to that problem. It also helps them to understand the importance of self-love and self-care.

Teaching love also helps children to understand and navigate the different forms of love and how to express them, which can help them to better understand and navigate the complexities of relationships. I like to refer to teaching love as the empathy seed. You help them understand the many forms of love and their knowledge of love becomes so heightened they can feel what's lacking in others and even evaluate when someone or something needs some love.

GIVING LOVE - This is the love that is expressed by providing for your child and meeting their needs, including material needs and emotional needs.

Giving love is important to a child's development because it helps to foster a sense of empathy, compassion, and generosity. When children are taught to give love and care for others, they learn to think about the needs and feelings of others, and develop a sense of empathy and compassion.

Additionally, giving love can also help children to develop a sense of responsibility and selflessness. They learn to put others' needs before their own and this can help to foster a sense of generosity. Giving love also helps children to develop social skills, such as communication and cooperation, which are important for forming healthy relationships.

Children who learn to give love and care for others may be more likely to develop a sense of purpose and meaning in life.

One of my favorite examples of this was shared by Philly rapper Tone Trump aka the Muslim Don on Episode 9 of the RAP DADS Podcast Vol. 1. He shared about a time he was leaving a store with his son and they came across a homeless woman panhandling. Tone instructed his son to give her some money. His son was reluctant, as any kid would be. His son questioned his father by saying, "But she's not Muslim." Tone explained to his son that while Muslims do look out for one another it doesn't exclude them from helping everyone who needs it. The son was obedient. Later that day while visiting Tone's mother, she blessed her generous grandson with twice the money he gave to the homeless woman. There are so many great lessons in giving love in that story.

UNCONDITIONAL LOVE - This is the big one. This is the love that is not based on any conditions or expectations, but is given freely and without reservation.

Unconditional love is important to a child's development because it also helps to provide a sense of security and self-worth. Children who feel unconditionally loved and accepted are more likely to develop a positive self-concept and self-esteem. They learn to trust themselves and others. Feeling unconditionally loved can help children to regulate their emotions and behavior, and can serve as a buffer against stress and negative experiences.

Unconditional love also helps children feel safe in expressing themselves and being themselves; this can be crucial for their emotional and psychological well-being. They learn that they are loved and accepted no matter what, which can help them to feel secure and confident in exploring their individuality. This can be important for children to have a sense of belonging and acceptance, which is huge.

Furthermore, children who feel unconditionally loved and accepted, may be more resilient in the face of adversity and more able to cope with the challenges of growing up. Unconditional love plays a crucial role in shaping a child's sense of self and the way they interact with others.

Now, this is obviously easier said than done but, TRY, TRY, TRY! At the end of the day we don't want to send our children out into the world seeking the type of love we failed to give them. Daddy issues aren't just for girls. Kendrick Lamar has a whole song about men with daddy issues (as mentioned in chapter one) and it's spot on. The way to ensure you're not leaving any vulnerabilities is to love on your kids every which way.

SPREAD LOVE NOT TRAUMA

Fellas, we can have a lot of trauma around love. Lack of specific types of love during certain times in our development can harden our hearts and even create lies we've used as defense mechanisms to cope with the pain. For the sake of your child search within yourself, identify them, and work them out so you don't pass it on to your next generation.

The mentality of, "I never had a father and I turned out fine" is a lie to cope with fatherlessness. I've spoken to a lot of men who grew up without a father and when the subject comes up, they always express how much they yearned for one. They knew something, or someone, was missing in their lives.

Side note: One of my favorite things to see is when men grow up and reach out to establish a relationship with their absent fathers. Like in the case of Jay-Z. He's spoken on many occasions[9], even on records, about his complicated relationship with his father. He ended up being understanding towards him given the unique circumstances his father was going through at the time he was a young boy. Can you imagine how healing that was for Jay?

It's worth mentioning that research shows the human body stores seven generations of trauma in our DNA. So we are not only fighting against the traumas we know but also traumas we didn't know existed in our lineage that haven't been worked through. This is why love is so important.

Back to the subject at hand. We can stop the continuation of generational curses and traumas by taking responsibility for our actions and working to break the patterns of behavior and thought that have been passed down through their family. We do this by:

1. Acknowledging and taking responsibility for any negative patterns or behaviors that have been passed down through our family.

2. Seeking help and support to address any personal issues or struggles that may be contributing to the continuation of generational curses and traumas. This may include therapy, counseling, or support groups.

3. Making a conscious effort to change negative patterns of behavior and thought, and adopting a more positive and healthy way of living.

4. Building strong and healthy relationships with our children, and modeling positive and healthy behavior for them.

5. Teaching and instilling healthy values, morals, and principles to our children, while encouraging them to be the best version of themselves.

6. Communicating and talking openly and honestly with our children about the family's history and the challenges that have been faced in the past.

7. Being involved in our children's lives and providing emotional support, guidance and love.

8. Encouraging our children to set and achieve personal goals, and to pursue their passions.

It's important to note that breaking generational curses and traumas is not something that can be done overnight. It requires consistent effort, time and patience, but it is possible with the right mindset and actions.

When I was young it didn't take me long to recognize how many of the men in my family, on both my mother's and father's sides, battled with substance abuse and mainly alcohol. I'd notice that my heroes would quickly turn into villains and the thing that took them from one extreme to the next was the bottle. This became the driving force in my quest to end that generational curse.

I took a stand for my future children that they would never have to experience what I did. This conscious decision impacted so many of my decisions. If I'd heard anything was "addictive" I'd stay away from it because of this conviction. I don't drink coffee because I overheard that it was addictive. I don't do any drugs, even the ones who don't have addictive qualities, because of this principle. This childhood experience had such a profound impact on me it had a hand in guiding the course of my life.

This is obviously an example of seeing something negative and wanting to shy away from it. But studies show the more normalized negative behavior is, the more desensitized you become[10] and it's highly likely that you too will engage in it.

I also made it a point not to become the sober dude pushing sobriety on everyone. My wife drinks and I have no problem with that whatsoever. Also, when it comes to my children, the decision to drink alcohol is totally up to them. I did make it a point to explain my position on drinking and drug use in hopes it would inspire them. But at the end of the day it's their lives and not mine. I'll love them anyway (see what I did there?).

Chapter Six

LEAD BY EXAMPLE

T his chapter will take the most "unlearning." So often we were taught that dad is the king of the castle. Dad gets the big piece of chicken. That's dad's chair, and so on. However, throughout history the best kings have been the ones who serve their subjects. These are the ones who get their hands dirty and earn the loyalty and admiration of their subjects.

We've all heard the phrase, "do as I say, not as I do." Well, I'm here to tell you, if you haven't figured it out for yourself by now, kids will do a little bit of both. The disclaimer doesn't completely absolve you or ensure your child won't follow your example.

One of the things I noticed early on about my father was that he was a hard worker. He worked two jobs during the week, another job on the weekend, and was an entrepreneur. My dad had a food truck business and would organize his siblings on major commercial "Hallmark" holidays, like Mother's Day and Valentine's Day, selling flowers on busy intersections in Philly. I remember helping out and making $300 in one weekend!

Though he never made it a point to explain why he worked so hard or the importance of hard work, I picked it up. When I became a husband and a father there was no excuse for my family being broke or going without. I learned just on the strength of the example I had of what a father is capable of.

When I got much older I asked my father why he worked so many jobs and discovered how many people relied on him to provide. It wasn't just me and my sisters, it was way more people than that. My father is a first generation immigrant. His parents came here from Puerto Rico with a third grade education. This also showed me selflessness. My father didn't turn his back on everyone, he stood strong and busted his ass so that we had what we needed.

My father is a brilliant medical scientist and graduated from the University of Pennsylvania so he did well for himself given his circumstances. To this day he works equally as hard as he did all those years. Only nowadays it's working for himself on the business he owns. Well, that and yard work. There's always a project in the back or front yard that keeps him busy.

BEWARE OF BAD HABITS

My son Esteban, the one I refer to as "my clone," had an amazing talent at picking up my bad habits and throwing them back in my face. I have a habit of slapping my wife on the butt every time I pass her. This was all good until one day my clone walked up behind my wife and slapped her on the butt and said, "gimme ba ba." For context, "ba ba" means bottle. She turned around and directly looked me in the eyes. My jaw dropped. The look on her face was that of defeat. I can't front. I still do it to this day. But for a while I had to stop.

There was another time when I was playing *Madden NFL*. I threw an interception and screamed at the TV, "What the fuck are you doing?" See, my receiver should have zigged but he zagged and that pissed me off. I'm a very passionate gamer, which is why I limit my access to video games.

Later on that day my mother called me and asked to speak to my son, Esteban. He grabs the phone and says, "Hey Me Mom, fuck you doing?" I turned white. Thank God my mom didn't understand him. But our reaction was enough to let him know he had something going. He'd continue to curse at everyone who came over to visit. And they all fell out laughing. He even turned it into a song. He would grab his toy piano and sing, "Whaaaatttt…the fuck you doingggg?" If viral was a thing in 2009, this kid would have been a smash!

Again, fatherhood is a mirror. It'll show you the good, the bad, and the ugly about yourself, if you're open enough to pay attention.

I GOT A STORY TO TELL…GANGSTERS MAKE THE BEST FATHERS PT. TWO

I remember being on the music video set for the 'High Hater Remix' by Maino. At this particular moment he had a smash hit record and was on top of the world.

The music video was set in his hometown of Brooklyn, New York. Maino arrives on set walking hand-in-hand with his son. As he navigated his way through the set, greeting people along the way, he was also introducing his son to the people he'd meet. I notice Maino made it a point to instruct his son how to introduce himself. To shake hands with his right hand only. To look the person in the eye when you meet them. Stuff like that. This is all happening in real time during his music video shoot day.

Talk about leading by example. This man took the time to not only bring his son along and expose him to his work and lifestyle, he also took the time and seized the opportunity at each teachable moment to guide his son.

Fathers can lead by example in many ways, including:

1. Modeling healthy relationships by treating our partners, children, friends, and family members with kindness, respect, and love.

   I remember one day my father pulled me aside and said, "I don't know how you have any friends the way you speak to people." This struck a chord in me because I valued my friends and would never want to offend them. But to be honest, I learned that from how he talks to his friends. All they do is clown one another. I thought that was normal. Nevertheless, he brought it to my attention and because it was something important to me I adjusted.

2. Being responsible and dependable in our roles as providers, caregivers, and decision-makers.

3. Showing Empathy and understanding towards others, and by actively listening to and valuing the perspectives and feelings of others

4. Encouraging education, reading and learning, and encouraging our children to do the same.
   This one is big for me. When I became a father I made it my purpose to re-brand the word "education." To most, the word means school. For me, it means learning. Period. My father changed my life when he told me I'd be a student for the rest of my life. And boy was he right. If i didn't seek out knowledge and information every day I'd be DONE.

   Just in my industry alone. When I came into the game it was all about cable tv and everything was shot on tapes. Three years later it was all about YouTube and everything went digital. Three years after that it was all about On Demand. Three years after that it was all about streaming services. If I stopped educating myself when I graduated college my skill set would be obsolete.

   Now when it comes to parenting, the same applies. Technology moves fast. Social norms change like the direction of the wind. The access to information our children have versus the encyclopedia set I had in my house is unfathomable. You'd better keep your head on a swivel and be on the lookout for new information to help you stay up to speed. What am I talking about? You're doing that right now with this book! Good job dads!

5. Being Active, maintaining a healthy lifestyle and eating a balanced diet.

6. Managing stress effectively, and by showing our children how to cope with stress in healthy ways.

7. Being a good role model, in terms of our behavior, attitude and values.

8. Being a good communicator, listening actively and expressing ourselves clearly and respectfully.

This one is huge. I've always been an advocate of explaining WHY I do things. If I'm upset, I explain to my kids why. This actually helped me a lot because my kids hate to disappoint me. So instead of having to yell and scream at them, I can just go to them and tell them why I'm disappointed. It strikes a nerve in them cause they never want to let me down.

I never use the phrase, "cause I said so." They don't get anything out of this. This also sets a tone and makes it acceptable for people to just tell them what to do without explanation. I'm raising kings not doormats.

9. Show kindness and generosity to others and encourage your children to do the same.

It is important to note that being a role model is not always easy, but it is a crucial part of being a father and it is a great way to positively influence the development of your children. Your kids will have role models. Wouldn't you rather it be you? Become the type of man your child would want to model themselves after.

Chapter Seven

DISCIPLINE

First and foremost I want to establish what I mean by "discipline." As you well know that word has many meanings. The definitions are as follows:

> **dis-ci-pline**
> Noun:
> The practice of training people to obey rules or a code of behavior,
> using punishment to correct disobedience.
> Verb:
> Train oneself to do something in a controlled and habitual way.

I believe that the noun definition leads to the verb definition, if that makes sense. Discipline is not a bad word and should not be presented in such a way. On the contrary, it is a beautiful word and a much needed skill/attribute to have if you are to be successful.

I like to think of the word in the earlier stages of life as structure. Life needs structure. It's the foundation on which we build. Teaching your child to clean up after themselves, be accountable and responsible, etc. are foundational principles. This is discipline! Once, and only once you've established that, you can rear or guide your child to remain on course.

This requires us fathers to be disciplined in our own lives. If you are someone going through life up to this point without structure, it's time to get discipline so you are not passing that haphazard lifestyle on to your child.

The beauty of a foundation of discipline is it helps to ensure your child is PROACTIVE and not REACTIVE. A life of structure is one with direction. When things are not going in the direction you want you can take notice and adjust. In a life without structure you are constantly reacting to what is going on. Things are just happening around you and you deal with it as it comes as opposed to charting the course of your life and forging ahead on that path.

I admit I was young and reckless. My coworkers would ask me things like, "How long were you trying to get pregnant?" As if it were planned. I realized right then and there that proactive people take the proper precautions to get out of life ONLY what they want. Here I was a mid-level member of the pull out gang and clearly wasn't good at it so a few got by the goalie. Don't cry for me. My little mistakes were the biggest blessings in the world. It set me on the fatherhood path and has been the most rewarding thing I've done in my life. Soon, if not now, you'll feel the same way.

ASS-WHOOPINS

Now let's address the elephant in the room, "To beat or not to beat, that. is the question." The answer? It's totally up to you.

I had a law I lived by. I would not beat my child until they were three years old. Before, and even after, they didn't really understand the consequences of their actions. Once they were smart enough to hear and understand, know it was on. I made the decision not to beat my sons when my youngest was three. I felt that I consistently bonded with my sons enough that I could talk to them or punish them if it came to that.

My older sons felt the sting of a leather belt in their lives. It did not occur often, but when I thought it was necessary. That's the important thing. No matter which side of the ass-whooping fence you fall on, make sure the punishment fits the crime. There's a thin line between beating and abusing. At the end of the day for me it was the age old question, would you rather be *LOVED* or *FEARED*? I chose love.

DISCIPLINE TIPS

The most effective way to discipline a child truly depends on the child's age, development, and individual needs. However, some general principles that are often considered effective include these examples:

1. *Consistency*: Establishing clear rules and consequences, and consistently enforcing them, can help children understand what is expected of them and what will happen if they don't follow the rules.

2. *Positive reinforcement*: Focusing on praising and rewarding positive behavior, rather than only punishing negative behavior, can help to encourage the child to continue making good choices. For some kids, all they want is attention. They'll act out if it means getting your attention. So give them some attention when they do well to counteract that impulse.

3. *Teaching problem-solving skills*: Teaching children how to identify and solve problems can help them to become more self-sufficient and responsible for their actions. Sometimes when our children come across a problem, it's easier for us to solve it for them or give them the answer. Doing this can deprive them of developing problem-solving skills. Encourage them to figure it out or help them work through it.

4. *Empathy*: Showing empathy and understanding towards your child's feelings and perspective helps them understand the impact of their actions on others. This can help to build trust and respect.

5. *Time-out*: Using a "time-out" as a consequence for misbehavior can be effective in helping children to calm down and reflect on their actions.

6. *Natural consequences*: Allowing children to experience the natural consequences of their actions can be effective in

helping them to learn and understand the importance of their behavior. When my sons became "tweens," I sat them down and prepared them for the next phase of their lives. I explained to them that their decision would have much greater consequences now that they were older and moving around more free and independently. Thank God they heeded my warning.

7. *Communication*: Open communication and active listening can help to build trust and understanding between you and your child, helping to address underlying issues that may be contributing to misbehavior.

It is important to note that effective discipline is not about punishment, but about teaching children how to make good choices, guiding them towards positive behavior and attitude. Again, it's important to consider the child's age and developmental level, as well as their individual needs and temperament when determining the most effective way to discipline.

"WHY," THE MISSING INGREDIENT

Take the time to explain to your children WHY they are being disciplined. Also take the time to make sure they understand why. If you are going through the trouble of disciplining without explaining why, you are just being abusive in my opinion. How will your child ever get the correlation between what they did and why it warranted disciplining?

R.I.P. to "Because I said so!"

DON'T STEAL OR SILENCE YOUR CHILD'S VOICE

It's important that we squash that old mentality of "children are to be seen and not heard." This lesson I learned from a neighbor of mine. He'd let his kid go crazy, "expressing himself." I asked why he let his kid talk to him that way and his answer shocked me. He encouraged his kids to speak their minds and not to bite their tongue, even if it meant he'd get the brunt of their fury. I adopted this philosophy but I tweaked it a bit.

I allow and encourage my kids to express themselves. I've learned that it often leads to meaningful conversation. My caveat is, the tone has to be respectful. My kids can say whatever they feel, as long as they do so with purpose and intention. When a child's voice is suppressed, it can have a number of negative effects on their physical, emotional, and social development.

Physically, when a child is not allowed to express themselves, they may experience stress, anxiety, and depression which can have negative effects on their overall health.

Emotionally, suppression of a child's voice can lead to feelings of low self-esteem, worthlessness, and a lack of trust in themselves and others. They may also have difficulty regulating their emotions, making them more prone to outbursts, anger, or withdrawal.

Socially, children whose voices are suppressed may have difficulty connecting with others and forming healthy relationships. They may also struggle to communicate effectively, which can lead to misunderstandings and conflicts in their interactions with others.

Every child deserves to be seen and heard.

I GOT A STORY TO TELL...ICE CUBE IS A COLD FATHER (in a good way)

I remember interviewing Ice Cube's son, O'Shea Jackson Jr. during the press run for the movie *Straight Outta Compton*. He told me how his father made him audition for the role. Ice Cube made him work for two years for the opportunity to play him in the film. He wanted to make sure his son had the discipline to take the part seriously and not feel entitled to it. *Straight Outta Compton* was a huge success and was O'Shea Jr.'s first role. But since then he's had a lot more and has turned acting into a real career path.

Chapter Eight

BE HUMAN

As we lead and guide our impressionable children, it's important to make sure they know we are human. By "human" I'm referring to not being perfect. It's very easy for a child to get the impression that we are. They look up to us. We are constantly advising them and pointing out their mistakes and shortcomings. That could lead their very impressionable, undeveloped minds into thinking we are perfect.

This can lead to all kinds of problems. Mainly with your child's self-esteem. Imagine the pressure of thinking you have to live up to perfection. Feeling like you have no room for error or mistakes. My wife and I always preached the following: "We do not demand perfection. We do expect your best."

I GOT A STORY TO TELL...PARENT SOMETIME UNDERSTAND

I grew up the middle child of two genius sisters. My older sister graduated high school at about fourteen or fifteen years old. My younger sister never got a "C" and was the youngest Vice Principal in New Jersey's history. I was a kid with a learning disability and a "C" student at best. Can you imagine the pressure!?!

My parents, eventually, understood that and encouraged me and developed my interests outside of school. Had their expectations been something I was incapable of, my life would have SUCKED! On the other hand, they never gave up on me nor would they let me give up on myself. They made sure I put in the effort.

APOLOGIZE TO YOUR CHILDREN WHEN YOU ARE WRONG...AND YOU WILL BE.

If I say or do something wrong I own up to it, in front of my kids. I do that to show them I'm human and to take accountability. There is no shame in that. When you don't own up to your mistakes you paint a false narrative that you are perfect or worse. You look stupid in front of your children who are smart enough to know you messed up and are trying to pretend you didn't. Now that's way more embarrassing than just facing the music.

On my *RAP DADS* podcast one of my favorite questions to ask the fathers I'm interviewing is about their biggest failure as a father. This one opens them up and forces them to come to terms with some of the most uncomfortable moments. You'd be surprised how many guests thank me for asking that question and feel relieved to get it off their chest.

I remember my biggest failure as a father. I was driving with my clone, Esteban Jr., who was about thirteen-years-old at the time. He was confiding in me about how sad he was for no reason. My son expressed how he was so down even though nothing seemed wrong. I began telling him how blessed he was and how he had nothing to be sad about because he lives such a great life. I was almost belittling him with how dismissive I was about his reality because I didn't see a reason for him to feel that way. Later on he shared with me how, in that moment, he was asking for help with his mental health. I completely blew it. More on this story in the next chapter.

Once I realized what I had done, I apologized to him profusely. Thank God we got him professional help. It could have been much worse. Our relationship had grown since that moment. I'm much more sensitive to his needs and our communication has gotten even deeper as a result.

Think of how many adults you know who harbor such resentment towards their parents for things that could have easily been resolved with an apology. My son could have easily felt that he couldn't trust or rely on me as a result of how I mishandled interpreting these warning signs. He had every right to feel that way.

Now that my sons are a bit older and more mature, I've also noticed they come to me and apologize when they do something wrong. Most young kids are trying to defend themselves or trying so hard not to get in trouble they deny, deny, deny. So when my sons come to me and fess up, I appreciate it. I know it's because I lead by example.

STOP TRYING TO BE GOD

You are not God. So don't act like it. Let them see God through you. The last thing you want is for your child to think you are God. To think you are their source or their savior. You will never live up to it because that is not your responsibility.

When you are someone's source, it's all good as long as you deliver, but the moment you can't it all comes crashing down. I interviewed Dame Dash and he said it best, "You can help someone over and over and over again. But the minute you tell them no or you can't help them, it's like you never did anything for them." It's impossible to be someone's source. So do yourself and more importantly your child a favor and don't even go there.

We also try so hard to protect our children that we often keep them from failing. We have the wisdom that comes from years and years of experience, so we can see things in their lives that they can't recognize. Although God gives us mercy and grace, he still allows us to be tested and fail. Failure is the best teacher.

Chapter Nine

KEEP AN OPEN MIND

When your kids are babies you have these fantasies about who they'll be when they grow up. Your one-year-old kid picks up a ball and throws it and you think you have an athlete on your hands. DO NOT fall into this trap. It will only lead you down a road of disappointment.

Some fathers look at their child and see all the dreams they never got to pursue. They project their lives onto this child. That's no way to lead either. Your child will either rebel and resent you or forever try to please you and never put themselves first.

You often hear first generation immigrants talk about their life growing up. Their own parents wanted them to be doctors and lawyers, but they wanted to be artists or creatives. This caused a huge issue for them, putting a toll on their relationship. Would you rather have an amazing relationship with your child or force them to live a life you want, only to have them hate you when they become adults?

I GOT A STORY TO TELL…THE GREATEST MC NEVER

At the age of about eight years old, my clone Esteban decided he wanted to be a rapper…and he was *gooood*. I'm a Hip-Hop journalist and a die-hard Rap fan. I dislike pretty much 99% of Hip-Hop artists and I can admit this kid was special. Google "TRNDSTTRS" and you can see and hear for yourself. He was performing on TV and even got paid to perform in LA for Live Nation. He was young, fly and super talented. He loved the spotlight and the spotlight loved him.

One day he decided he didn't want to rap anymore and wanted to take his music in the Punk Rock direction. I was crushed. This kid was so good at such a young age. He was only going to get better. He made a young Li'l Bow Wow look like a pup in comparison to his skills and performance ability. No disrespect to Bow Wow. He is a legend and deserves his flowers. This is how impressed I was with my son's talent.

I had to quickly put my own wants for him aside and support him on his new journey. I had to be all in. I still think about what a tragedy it is that the world will never get to hear this amazing MC but when I see him on stage in his element, performing the music he loves, I know he made the right decision.

Your open-minded support will not only help your relationship with your child but it will help your child with forming healthy relationships of their own. To the fellas with daughters, you wouldn't want them to grow up and choose a partner who forces their will onto them because you did it to your daughter. She feels like this is not only acceptable but a sign of love. I've spoken to women who sadly live this reality.

Fellas with sons, you wouldn't want your son to grow up and take any type of treatment from his superiors at work because you treated him that way and now he's normalized it.

Like it or not, you are the first "authority figure" in your child's life. Being open-minded will demonstrate the type of leadership they should be seeking out and will help not to normalize dictatorships.

Here are some ways you can be open-minded to your child:

1. Listening actively to what your child has to say, without interrupting or judging, and trying to understand their perspective.

   This one goes back to the story I told you in the last chapter about my biggest failure as a father. Had I been listening to my son with the goal of understanding his perspective when he was trying to tell me he needed help with his mental health, I would have caught it and been able to help sooner.

2. Encourage open communication by creating an environment where your children feel comfortable expressing themselves, asking questions, and sharing their thoughts and feelings.

   My father created a space for us to have deep private conversations. We would get in the car and just ride. That was our safe space. I could tell him anything and he would just listen and help me work it out. I highly suggest that.

3. Be non-judgmental, avoid making quick judgments or as-

sumptions about your child's thoughts, feelings, or actions. Instead try to understand where they are coming from.

This one is an expert level rule. In the moment, be cool and calm, leading with love. If you snap, you could be throwing away a lifetime of love and relationship.

To go even deeper I think here you can employ the , "choose your battles" method. Sometimes in order to win the war you have to lose a few battles. Some losses aren't final. Choose wisely.

4. Encourage independence and allow your child to make their own decisions. Allow them to take responsibility for their actions.

I remember a time where my oldest son wasn't being in- cluded by his normal crowd of friends. It was basketball season and they all joined a team and didn't include him. I told him we could go to them and ask to be on their team or we can read the writing on the wall and join a different team. It was tough for him to play with kids he didn't know against a team full of his "friends." But in the end he got to see their true colors. More importantly he learned how to be independent and not rely on a crowd for validation. Today I'm convinced you can drop that kid anywhere and he'll make new friends and find his way.

5. Be open to learn and grow alongside your child, and be open to feedback and constructive criticism.

It's inevitable that we will learn and grow as fathers. If you are the same man when your child was born as you are when they graduate high school, something is wrong. Just as excited as you are to teach them new things, be just as excited to learn a few new things from them.

It's important to note that being open-minded doesn't mean that you should neglect your role as an authority figure, or be permissive. Rather, it's about being willing to listen, consider and respect the perspectives and feelings of your child, which is crucial for the child's emotional and psychological well-being.

Chapter Ten

HAVE FAITH

On this fatherhood journey, the road is filled with so much uncertainty. There are so many blind spots. There's much that's out of your control, your only hope is to have faith. If not you will go crazy or overcompensate by trying to control everything and ruin your child's life.

Again, I'm not a religious man, I'm a spiritual one. I believe in God because of my experience, not because I was told to. The evidence is crystal clear just in my life as it pertains to fatherhood.

When I was young my mother and father were not together. They didn't get back together until I was eight years old. I didn't know that would play a part in the empathy and understanding I'm able to show my oldest son who experienced the same situation when my wife decided to leave his father. I knew what it felt like to go from Mommy's house to Daddy's house on the weekends. I was able to tap into that when I came into his life and help him through that experience.

I grew up creative. Everything I saw was an instrument or tool for me to use to get my thoughts out. I was able to use that experience and create an environment for my creative sons to flourish. I know what I needed when I was in their positions, so I can tap into that experience and support them in ways most parents can't.

These may seem like situations that happen by coincidence but I know they happened by design. God knew I'd be a step-father. He knew I'd be the father of creatives so he planted those experiences so I'd have a point of reference. I say all that to say, include God in your fatherhood journey, no matter what God you believe in or pray to. You'll need all the help you can get.

I GOT A STORY TO TELL...GOD DID!

In 2010, I took a job as Chris Brown's live-in videographer. At the time my sons were six years old, three years old and six months old. I originally turned the project down because I didn't want to be away from them. My wife convinced me to take it because it was an amazing opportunity, and would be a career booster, so I did. She was absolutely right.

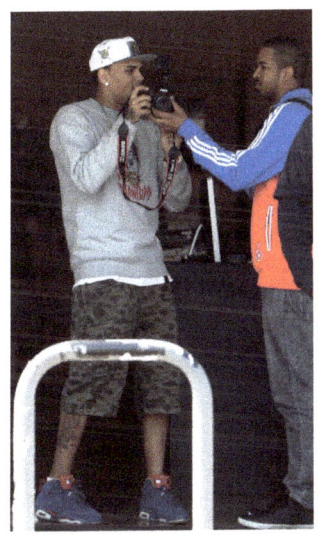

My first destination was Miami. Chris was recording at the Hit Factory for a couple of weeks. I boarded the plane and off I went. As soon as I opened the door to my hotel room I fell to my knees. It hit me like a ton of bricks that I was a long way from home. I heard God whisper in my ear, "Now, you have no choice but to trust me." I started balling my eyes out. Up and to that point I was always in arms reach. Now, I'm thousands of miles away and could not mobilize immediately back to them even if I wanted to. He was right. I had to trust him.

To be honest looking back on it, even in arms reach, some things are just out of your control. Don't let proximity fool you. We are always trusting God. Now I was face to face with it.

That moment freed me and allowed me to focus on my project knowing God had my back.

SPIRITUAL SPIDEY SENSES

Moms have that intuition. It's crazy but so true. I remember so many times when my mom knew something without any evidence.

I remember coming home after I lost my virginity and my mom was in the living room crying. I asked her what was wrong and she said, "I know you had sex for the first time." I was floored. How on God's green earth did she know that?

Another time, when I was an adult, I woke up in the middle of the night with a sharp pain in my stomach. I rolled out of my bed onto the floor in agonizing pain. The next day my mother called me to check on me. She said she was woken up out of her sleep in the middle of the night and just started praying for me. I can list a lot more of these types of examples but you get the point.

As fathers, we don't have that connection. However, I have the illest work-around - God.

I remember it was freshman year of high school for my oldest son, JoJo. He was going to this amazing magnet school. One morning he was moving around a bit slow and heavy. As he went to grab the door knob to leave, God told me to hug him. I did. My son melted into my arms and began to cry. Turns out he put a lot of pressure on himself with his grades. Progress reports were coming out later that week and he was concerned. I assured him that he was fine and that no matter what the report said it wasn't the end of the world and he could fix it if needed. He left the house reassured. Later on the progress report came in and turns out he was killing it. The kid graduated high school in the National Honors Society.

Thankfully I built a relationship with God and included him in my parenting. I was able to be there for my son even when he didn't ask for it.

I pray for my sons and my family daily. It's a simple prayer. It goes a little something like this:

> God, thank you for blessing me with an amazing family. Thank you for trusting me to nurture and protect them. Thank you for providing for them through me. Now, I want to invite you to be part of my life as a father and a husband. Please guide me in my decision making. Please point out things I may miss or overlook. Please send your angels to protect my sons, my wife and my dogs. Please keep the whole family happy and healthy. Amen.

Spirituality can help parenting in several ways. Examples include: providing a sense of purpose and meaning, encouraging mindfulness, teaching values and morals, helping cope with stress, promoting gratitude and appreciation and providing guidance.

It's important to note that spirituality can mean different things to different people and can be practiced in many ways. It can be through religion, personal beliefs, or practices like meditation or mindfulness. Additionally, spirituality can be an individual or a shared experience, and it can be an important aspect of parenting. For me, it's the ultimate cheat code.

1. Institute For Research On Poverty , "Involved Fathers Play An Important Roles An Important Role In Children's Lives," University of Wisconsin-Madison, February 2020

2. The Fresh Prince of Bel-Air, Season 4, Episode 24, "Papa's Got a Brand New Excuse," directed By Shelley Jensen, Aired May 9, 1994, NBC.

3. Duckworth, Kendrick Lamar, "Father Time," Track 5 on Mr. Morale and The Big Steppers, pgLand, 2022

4. Fuse, "A$AP Rocky Slams XXL Freshman Class - SXSW," Interviewed by Esteban Serrano, March 15, 2012, 3:27

5. Courtney Seiter, "The Psychology of Social Media: The Deep Impulses That Drive Us Online," Buffer, August 10, 2016

6. K. Magnuson and L. M. Berger, "Family Structure States and Transitions: Associations with Children's Well-Being during Middle Childhood," Journal of Marriage and Family 71 (2009): 575–591.

7. Kendrick Lamar, Good Kid, M.A.A.D City Album, Top Dawg Entertainment, Aftermath Entertainment and Interscope Records. 2012

8. Jane Kelly, "We Asked An Expert Why We Hold Hands, And Learned It's Good For You," UVA Today, , (February 13, 2020).

9. Jay-Z, The Black Album Interview, By Sway Calloway, MTV, 2003

10. Anjana Madan, Slyvie Mrug, Michael Windle, "Emotional Desensitization to Violence Contributes to Adolescents' Violent Behavior," Journal of Abnormal Child Psychology, January 2016,

CONCLUSION

Fatherhood is a journey that requires preparation, patience, and a willingness to learn and grow. As a person who loves Rap music, I've come to realize that many of the themes and messages from Hip-Hop culture can be applied to fatherhood. Key aspects include the importance of being a role model, to the importance of being open-minded and understanding, to the importance of being a provider, protector, and teacher. The lessons of fatherhood can be found in the lyrics of many of our favorite Rap songs.

It's not just about the lyrics, it's also about the mindset, the attitude, and the spirit of Hip-Hop. The determination, resilience, and the ability to overcome obstacles that are often celebrated in Rap music are also essential for fatherhood. It's about being the best version of yourself and striving to be a better father, day by day.

Being a father is not easy, it's a challenging and rewarding journey that requires patience, persistence and love. With the right mindset, attitude and approach, you can be the best father you can be.

I hope you enjoyed this book. I hope I was able to paint a more vivid picture of what this journey will be like and also, hopefully, provide some insight to help you navigate. If anything, use this book as a fresh perspective and not so much as a step-by-step *booklet*.

Your paternal instincts will guide you along. As long as your heart and mind are pure, you will be fine. Oh, and remember, ""Whatever is best for the child, wins."

God Bless you and your family. Enjoy the journey. Peace.